Can  play here?

Tug, tug, tug!

Are the [dolphins] at play?

[Dolphins] can hit the [balls].

Can a pig play at a pit?
The pig dug a big, big pit.

Can a [squirrel] dig?

It can dig for a big, big nut.

And it can jump!

Can  play?

Get set to jump!

 can play and get wet.

Can a fox fit here?

It can play at the den.

The big, big is hot.
But can it play?
It can get wet, wet, wet!

Can play?
Get set for a big, big hug!

Animals like to play.